Myths and Legends 3

**Harry Stanton
and Audrey Daly**

Oliver & Boyd

*Illustrated by Irene Barry, Donald Harley, John Harrold,
Tony Herbert, Annabel Large, Michael Strand, Gwen Tourret
and Shirley Tourret.*

Oliver & Boyd
Robert Stevenson House
1–3 Baxter's Place
Leith Walk
Edinburgh EH1 3BB

A Division of Longman Group Ltd

First published 1983

ISBN 0 05 003362 X

© Oliver & Boyd 1983

Printed in Hong Kong by
Wing King Tong Co. Ltd

Preface

Every country has its own oral traditions of myth and legend, and the stories in this series come from the four corners of the earth. They will help the modern child to appreciate how happenings may be interpreted in different ways by people whose entire way of thinking may, for many reasons, be different.

The series is intended for an age range of 7 + to 11 + , with more easily understood stories in the first two books and more difficult concepts in the two later books.

Harry Stanton
Audrey Daly

Contents

Winter and Summer

Once upon a time, there was no winter or summer.

Flowers were always in bloom, and fruit was ready to be picked all through the year.

The goddess who ruled over all the plants of the earth was Demeter. She made rain when it was needed for the plants to grow, and she made sure the corn was ripe so that no one went hungry.

Demeter was a happy, gentle goddess, and she had a beautiful daughter called Persephone.

Persephone was so beautiful that Hades, the king of the underworld, fell in love with her. He wanted to marry her, but he knew that Demeter would never let her daughter go to live in the grim underworld with him.

So each day, he watched and waited for a chance
to capture the lovely young girl. Persephone never
saw his black chariot with its four black horses,
for Hades always stayed hidden in the trees.

Then one day, when Persephone and some of her
friends were picking flowers, Persephone saw a
strange flower that she had never seen before. She
left her friends and went to look at it—and Hades
saw his chance. He shook the reins and his horses
moved softly towards Persephone.

She did not hear the chariot. Just as she bent
down to look at the strange flower, Hades leaned
out of his chariot and dragged her in.

Persephone cried out as they galloped away,

but the chariot did not stop. Faster and faster
they galloped, until at last Hades struck the earth
with his spear. A deep hole appeared, leading to
the underworld where Hades was king.

Just as the chariot raced below the earth,
Persephone threw her golden belt into a nearby
stream.

"Perhaps when my mother is looking for me,"
she thought, "she will find the belt."

Demeter heard Persephone's last cry for help,
but she did not know where her daughter had gone.

Night and day she searched, all over the world,
calling her daughter's name. Week after week,
month after month, she looked, until one day she
stopped by a waterfall and saw Persephone's golden
belt lying in the stream near by.

As Demeter sat by the waterfall she heard the
voice of the stream.

"Persephone is deep in the underworld. She is
Hades' Queen, and she looks very sad."

Now Demeter knew where her daughter was—but
she also knew that there was nothing she could do to
help her. No one who went into the underworld
ever came out again.

Demeter sat thinking hard. The only one who

could help was Zeus, the father of the gods—and he would not help because Hades was his brother.

After thinking for a long time, Demeter knew that there was only one way she could get Zeus to help. She went into a deep cave and stayed there. She knew that as long as she was in the cave, there would be no one to look after the plants of the earth, no rain would fall and nothing would grow.

So Demeter remained in the cave. No rain fell, the plants began to wither and the leaves began to fall. Soon even the grass began to die, so that there was no food for men or animals to eat.

Then people cried out to Zeus to help them, for they were growing hungry. Zeus sent many messengers to Demeter, asking her to make the crops grow again, but she took no notice until Zeus came to see her himself.

"I will make the plants grow again when Persephone comes back to me," she said.

"Persephone may return to the earth if she hasn't eaten anything while she has been in the underworld," said Zeus.

Then he sent Hermes, his messenger, to bring Persephone back to her mother, who was overjoyed to see her.

Now while Persephone had been in the underworld, she had been so unhappy that she could not eat anything at all. But only that morning, she had suddenly felt hungry and she had eaten six pomegranate seeds. When Zeus heard this, he said that she must spend six months of each year in the underworld—a month for each seed.

So each year, when Persephone comes back to earth, the grass and leaves spring from the earth, the corn grows high and summer comes again.

And when she returns to the underworld, her mother Demeter goes sadly back to her cave.

There is no one to look after the growing things, so the leaves fall and the year fades into winter—until Persephone returns once more, in the springtime.

The World's Wisest Man

Alfonso Claudius Crabbe was a tramp. He had
wandered the highways and byways of Italy for many
years. When he was hungry, he begged for his food,
and at night he would sleep in the barn of a friendly
farmer or under a hedge.

Often he went without food, and his clothes
were any he could find. None of them fitted him,
and they were all tattered and torn.

It was many years since he had slept in a soft bed,
and he knew another cold winter was approaching.

"If only I could find a warm home for the
winter," he thought as he sat in the thin watery
sunlight of late autumn. He shook his begging
bowl at a passing stranger, but no money was
dropped into the bowl.

"This is a mean town," he muttered to himself.

At that moment a herald walked into the town
square, and two trumpeters blew a fanfare.

"Hear ye, hear ye!" cried the herald. "The
king has lost a valuable ring, worth many thousand
lire. It was a present from the king of Persia,
so a reward of as much gold as a man can carry
will be given to the man who can tell the king

10

where the ring is hidden."

"Surely the king has plenty of wise men and astrologers who can tell him where the ring is?" said a bystander.

"All the wise men have tried, without success," replied the herald. "All their skill and all their knowledge is of no use. They stayed at the palace for many months, but none of them could find the ring."

When Alfonso Claudius Crabbe heard that, it occurred to him that he could offer to find the ring. No harm would come to him if he failed, and if he did find it, he would be rich for the rest of his life.

So the very next day he presented himself at the palace gates.

"Tell the king that Alfonso Claudius Crabbe has come to help him to find the ring which he has lost," he said to one of the palace guards.

Trying to look very important in his tattered rags, he was taken before the king, who looked disdainful when Crabbe was brought into the throne room.

"And how can a dirty, ragged tramp help me?" asked the king in a haughty voice.

"Forgive the state of my clothes, O king, but when I am thinking I care little for what I am wearing," replied Alfonso.

"Then tell me where my ring is hidden," demanded the king.

"I shall need time to study the problem," said Alfonso. "I only heard about it this morning."

"You will be given one month to solve the problem," said the king. "During that time you will stay at the palace, and the finest books on astrology and magic will be there for you to consult. Anything you need will be found—especially a new suit of clothes," finished the king, wrinkling his nose.

After the royal tailor had fitted him with a new suit of clothes, Alfonso Claudius Crabbe was shown to a room near the royal library, where he could look at all the books of magic and astrology. He spent most of the day looking at them, although he could neither read nor write. He scribbled all over huge sheets of paper so that the servants would think he was taking notes.

He enjoyed the food, and the comfort of a soft bed. When the servants or the king's courtiers came into his room, he would stare grimly at them, or pretend to be thinking so deeply that he did not notice them.

Some of the servants looked over his shoulder as he wrote his notes.

"He writes in a strange language," they told one another. "He must be a very wise man."

Crabbe hardly ever spoke to the servants, and they began to feel very uneasy. It was they who had taken the king's ring, and each time Crabbe stared at them, they felt guilty. Some of them began to call him, "Wise Sir", or "My Lord Wizard", and Crabbe began to get suspicious. The more he thought about their behaviour the more certain

he became that the servants knew where the king's ring was hidden.

Now he needed some help, so he sent for his sister. He smuggled her into his room and hid her under his bed. He told her that each time a servant came into the room, she was to cry out in a high-pitched whisper, "That is one of them."

The servants could not see Crabbe's sister, they could only hear the voice.

"It's a spirit voice," one said. "A demon conjured up by the wizard," muttered another. "We're the only people to have heard the voice," moaned a third.

"What shall we do?" they asked one another.

"We must give him the ring and beg for mercy," said the most sensible of the servants.

"And we must take him a present," said another.

Quickly they hurried to his room. "We know that you know that we stole the ring," said one of the servants. "Here it is." And he handed the ring to Alfonso Claudius Crabbe.

Crabbe took the ring and said nothing. He just stared grimly back at them.

"We have also brought you a present," said another servant, handing him a small bag of gold.

"We have no more money," cried the oldest servant. "Please do not tell the king that we stole his ring."

"Very well," said Crabbe. "I will accept the gold. It will be my reward for saving your lives. Now you must do exactly as I tell you."

He pointed to a turkey strutting across the courtyard. "Take the ring, and when you feed the turkey this evening, put the ring in the bird's food. When it has swallowed the ring, come and tell me."

The servants could hardly believe their ears. It seemed such a strange order, but that evening when they fed the turkey, they placed the ring in the bird's food. As soon as the turkey had swallowed the ring, one of the servants went and told Crabbe, who immediately went to see the king.

"Sire," he said, "I know where your ring is hidden. After studying for almost a month, the stars have revealed to me the exact place."

The king was astonished. "Where? Where?" he demanded.

Crabbe pointed to the turkey as it strutted across the courtyard in the early evening sunlight. "There is the thief. That turkey stole your ring. It is in the crop of that bird."

The wise men and courtiers with the king all burst out laughing.

The king did not laugh, but he said, "If this is a silly joke, then you will suffer."

"There's only one way to find out," said Alfonso Claudius Crabbe.

So the bird was killed—and, just as Crabbe had foretold, the ring was in its crop.

The courtiers and wise men and astrologers all kept very quiet. Suddenly they were afraid of Crabbe and his magic.

The king of course was delighted. Not only did he double the reward, but he ordered a special banquet to honour Alfonso Claudius Crabbe.

The head cook decided to make a special soup, a soup with all kinds of fish in it. That night he made it even richer than usual by adding some crab meat. Only the king and the cook knew that the crab meat had been added.

As the most important guest at the banquet, Alfonso Claudius Crabbe sat next to the king.

"Tell me," said the king, "what do you think of the soup?"

"It is excellent soup," replied Crabbe.

"Since you are such a wise man, you will be

able to tell me what special ingredient makes this
soup so good," said the king.

Poor Alfonso was bewildered. He had no idea
what was in the soup. And if he could not say,
they would all stop thinking how clever he was.

He muttered to himself—just as he used to when
he was a tramp—"Crabbe, you are in trouble.
Crabbe, you are in the soup!"

"Bravo! Bravo!" shouted the king. "You really
are the world's wisest man!"

And Alfonso Claudius Crabbe smiled a wise smile,
and said not one more word.

Grandmother Spider Catches the Sun

There are many different tribes of Indians in North America—Sioux, Cheyenne, Cherokee, Blackfoot and so on—all with their own rich funds of stories from the past. The following story is told by the Cherokee.

*　　*　　*　　*　　*　　*

Long long ago, at the beginning of time, it was dark. No one could see where they were going, and the animals kept bumping into one another, and falling off rocks and into rivers.

The fox grew very tired of it. "If there was some light, we would be able to see one another, and we would be able to see what we were doing," he said to everyone he bumped into.

After a while all the other animals grew tired of not being able to find their way about, so they called a meeting to talk about the matter.

The red-headed woodpecker was the first to speak.

"I've been told," he said, "that there are people living on the other side of the world who have this thing called light. It lights up the darkness, and all the people can see one another."

"Then why haven't *we* got any?" asked the wolf.

"I don't know, but perhaps if we went there and asked, the people might give us some of their light so that we can see too," replied the woodpecker.

All the other animals thought that the woodpecker spoke wisely, but the fox was not so sure.

He said, "These people have had all the light to themselves for so long that I don't think they'll give us any. I think it would be better if one of us went and stole a piece of this light without the people knowing."

"That's a very good idea!" agreed the bear. "I'll go and steal some. I'm big and strong, so I shall be able to carry as much of this light as you want."

"Oh no," said the snake. "The trouble with you is that you are *too* big. The people will hear you and see you. You won't be able to steal any light without being noticed."

"If the bear is too big, who would be best?" asked the other animals.

"Let *me* try," said the possum with the bushy tail. "They won't notice me, and when I steal a piece of this light, I can hide it under my fur."

So the possum was sent to get some light. His

journey was long and difficult, but as he hurried along, it began to get lighter and lighter. At first the light was very faint, but as he travelled further it became brighter and brighter, and the possum had to screw up his eyes. He went on until he saw the sun.

"So that's where it all comes from!" he said, astonished. He crept up to the sun and broke off a tiny piece. He hid it in his bushy tail, then set off for home.

Possum had never seen the sun before, so he did not know anything about it. Of course the sun was very hot, and even the little piece that possum had hidden in his tail burned him. But he was a brave

little animal, and he did not want the other animals to think that he was afraid. He kept on running with his tail held high.

"Here I am," he shouted when he got home.

When the animals came hurrying up, they looked and looked, but there was no light to see by.

They could smell burning, for the sun had burned the fur on possum's bushy tail. Now it was quite bare, and possums have never had fur on their tails since that day.

Worst of all, the tiny piece of sun which the possum had stolen had burned itself up, and it had gone out.

"Now let *me* try," said the eagle. "I have more sense than the possum. I shall put the light on my head and fly back here with it."

So the eagle flew off into the darkness to look for light. In time he found the place where it was light, and not long afterwards he saw the sun.

The people there were keeping an eye on their sun, because they had noticed that a piece had been stolen. They saw the eagle when he dived down and stole a piece and put it on his head.

It was not long before he discovered, just as the possum before him had discovered, that the sun was

very, very hot. The sun burned his head, just as it
had burned the possum's tail.

"Oh!" he cried. "My head is being burnt!"
But he did not throw the piece of sun away, in
case the other animals would think that he was
afraid.

When he reached home, the light had gone out.
But the sun had burned all the feathers off the top
of his head and left him bald—just like the
bald-headed eagle looks today.

"You are no better than the possum!" said the
fox. "We shall always have to live in the dark."

"Perhaps I can help," said a small voice. It was
the little old grandmother spider. "I will go and
steal a piece of the sun."

"Very well," agreed the animals. "You go this
time."

The spider went to the river-side and found a
small piece of damp clay. "This is what I need,"
she said, and she made the clay into a little round
bowl. Then she set off, spinning a thread behind her,
so that she would know the way home.

When she reached the place where it was light,
the people were watching the sky in case the eagle
came back, and they did not see the tiny spider.

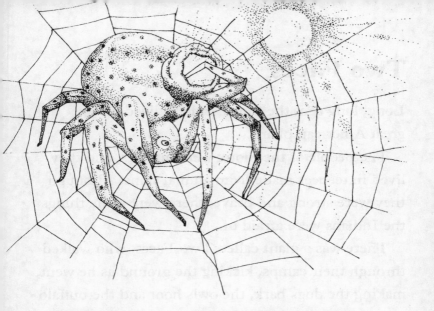

She went up to the sun, broke off a tiny piece, and put it in her bowl. Then she turned and ran back along the thread, while the tiny piece of sun still burned in her bowl.

"Here comes the light!" shouted all the animals as she returned. "Now we can see!" And they looked at one another, very pleased.

"Can you see this as well?" asked the spider, and she showed them the tiny round bowl which the sun had baked as hard as a rock.

"That will be very useful!" said the animals.

And that is how the little old grandmother spider captured the sun, and how she discovered how to make clay bowls.

Two Faces

Long, long ago, the Sioux Indians lived on the great American plains.

The people of the Sioux were hunters, and they lived in teepees made from animal skins. Although they were strong and brave, there were some things the Indians were afraid of.

There was a giant called Two Faces, who walked through their camps, kicking the ground as he went, making the dogs bark, the owls hoot and the buffalo stampede. The giant Two Faces had such great ears that each of them was large enough to hold three men. All the Indians were terrified of him for many years, until at last he was killed by a man and his wife whose child he had stolen.

The child was a naughty boy who argued and would never do as he was told. At last, one night, his mother was so angry that she said,

"If you won't do as you're told, I will put you outside and the giant Two Faces will put you into his ear."

The little boy went on arguing, so his mother pushed him out of the teepee into the cold night air. For a little while, the boy ran round and round the teepee, laughing and shouting, as small children will. Then suddenly his cries of joy stopped. He gave a cry of fear, and then he was heard no more.

His mother grew anxious, and ran outside to find him, but he had gone. For many days she and her husband searched and wept for their son, until one night she heard a voice outside their teepee say, "I must find another little boy."

The wife said to her husband, "I am sure that the giant Two Faces has taken our little boy. Tomorrow we must try to get our son back."

The following night she hid behind the woodpile and waited. In the moonlight, she heard something marching through the camp. She peeped out and

saw a huge figure coming towards her. It stopped beside her teepee.

Fear filled her heart, but she remembered her son and grew brave. She ran out and seizing one of the monster's legs, shouted for her husband. Together they tied the giant with thongs, then killed him with an axe.

When dawn broke, they saw what they had killed. It was a most hideous giant, covered from neck to toes with thick black hair.

Taking the axe, they split open the creature's ears, and inside, they found their son. He was very thin and unable to speak, and there was a thick coat of long black hair all over his body.

If they had not rescued him, he would have become another Two Faces monster.

For many weeks the little boy lay in his parents' teepee, near to death. But with the loving care of his mother and the magic herbs of the medicine man, he was saved.

This was the story that all Sioux mothers told to their children, to help to make them good.

Jeannie of Dumfries

From John o' Groats and the great mountains of the
north to Hadrian's Wall and the gentler hills of the
south, Scottish folktales abound. They tell of battles,
heroes, strange monsters, and brave, strong-minded
women such as the heroine of this story.

★   ★   ★   ★   ★   ★

Everyone thought that Jeannie of Dumfries was the
most beautiful of all the girls in the Border country
between Scotland and England. Jeannie took great
care of her lovely skin and each morning, as the first
rays of sunshine lit up the sky, she went into the
garden to wash her face in the morning dew.

Then one morning Jeannie went into the garden—
and she didn't come back. Her parents and her sister
Mary searched first the garden and then the
countryside around for many hours. But she had
vanished as if she had never been there at all.

"Whatever could have happened to her?" cried
Jeannie's mother. "She is such a good girl. She would
never run away!"

"She must be somewhere," declared her father.
"We will get a search party together to find her."

So for many weeks, men looked far and wide for Jeannie. Barns, woods and moorlands were all searched, but not a trace of her could be found.

"A witch or a wizard—or perhaps the fairies—must have stolen her away," sobbed Jeannie's mother.

"If that is so, I will go and get her back," said Mary, Jeannie's sister. "*I'm* not frightened of witches or wizards or fairies. They won't harm *me*."

Mary's parents did not want her to leave the house to look for Jeannie. They were afraid that she too might disappear.

"Please let me go and look for her," pleaded Mary. "Otherwise, I shall never smile again!" she vowed. So at last she was allowed to go and look for her sister.

Before Mary left home, her father gave her a small bag with some gold in it. Her mother gave her a golden needle, a silver thimble and a packet of pins.

Mary spent many weeks hunting for her sister Jeannie, without success. Then one day she met a traveller who told her, "I have seen your sister. The wicked wizard who lives in Talisman Castle holds her prisoner. If I were you, I would keep away. If he sees you, he will lock you up as well!"

When Mary heard that Jeannie was still alive, she was overjoyed. She set off straightaway to save her sister from the wicked wizard.

For many days she walked across the hills and glens, until at last she saw Talisman Castle in the mist at the top of a steep hill. The castle had grim black walls, and all around it was silent and still, with not even a bird singing.

A shiver went down Mary's spine as she looked up at her sister's prison. And as she stared upward, she heard a clinking sound behind her. Turning round, she saw a tinker pulling a cart loaded with pots, pans and kettles.

When he came up to her, Mary asked, "Why are you walking between the shafts of that cart?"

"I'm so poor that I have to pull my own cart," said the tinker. "I shall never have enough money to buy a horse."

Mary was a very kind-hearted girl. She took out her purse and said, "You need a horse to pull that heavy cart. Take this gold and buy one for yourself."

"I cannot take your money!" said the tinker.

"I shall not need it," Mary replied. "The gold was to help me to find my sister, and now I know where she is. She is held prisoner in that castle up there, and I'm going to rescue her."

"Then I will accept your gift," said the tinker, "for it is the kindest thing that has ever happened to me in all the years that I have been a tinker. In return, when you go into the castle, remember these words—a pure heart is never afraid."

Mary thanked the tinker and set off up the hill, repeating his words to herself.

She had not gone very far when she met a poor beggar going the other way. His clothes were badly torn, and he was trying to fasten them together with thorns.

"You poor man!" cried Mary. "Thorns won't hold

your clothes together." She looked into her bag and found the packet of pins which her mother had given her. "Take these," she said. "They will be of no use to me when I go into the castle to rescue my sister."

"Thank you, my dear," said the beggar. "It is many years since I met anyone so kind. In return, when you go into the castle, remember these words— gold and silver will save you from evil."

Mary went on up the hill, puzzling over these strange words. At last she reached the great black door of the castle and banged loudly on it. From inside she could hear footsteps, then the door creaked slowly open. There stood the ugliest man Mary had ever seen in her life. It was the wizard!

"What do you want?" he growled, staring down at her with his evil red eyes.

"I have come for my sister!" said Mary bravely.

"Your sister?" smiled the wizard, showing large pointed yellow teeth. "Come in, and I will see if I can find her."

Inside the castle it was very gloomy. As the wizard slammed the big door, the sound echoed hollowly.

"Wait here, and I will try to find your sister," said the wizard, and he went off with a grim chuckle.

Mary grew colder and colder as she waited in the dark hall. Then suddenly she heard strange sounds. She saw ghostly shapes around her, wailing and shrieking.

"Go away, go away! Run, run, run!" they seemed to be saying.

At first Mary was frightened. Then she remembered the tinker's words—"A pure heart is never afraid."

"The wizard is trying to frighten me away so that I won't be able to rescue Jeannie," she said to herself. She stood bravely and faced the ghosts, and in a few moments they were gone.

When the wizard came back after a while, he was very surprised to find Mary still there. He thought for a moment, then he said, "Come with me. There are many girls in this castle. If you can find your sister among them, then you can both leave. But if you cannot find her, you too will have to stay here for ever." He rubbed his hands together as he spoke, enjoying the thought.

He led Mary into another large hall. This one was lit by flickering torches fixed to the walls, and along one side there were twelve white statues. Every single one looked like Mary's sister Jeannie!

"If you tell me which is your sister," cackled the wizard, "you can both leave."

Mary looked at the statues. They were all exactly alike, and she knew that she must make no mistake. Then the words of the beggar came back to her – "Gold and silver will save you from evil."

From her bag, Mary took the silver thimble which her mother had given her. She placed it carefully upon the finger of the first statue. And the thimble turned black! Mary tried all the other statues, one by one, and the same thing happened. At last she came to the last one. When she placed the thimble upon the finger of the last statue, the thimble shone with a bright silvery light.

"Here is my sister!" cried Mary – and as she spoke, the statue changed back into her sister, just as beautiful as always.

The wizard gave a scream of rage and stepped towards Mary and Jeannie.

Hand in hand, they ran from the room and fled through the long corridors to the great door of the castle. They tugged at the handle, and the door opened to let them through.

As they rushed breathlessly down the steep hillside, they heard an angry screech above them. It was the wizard in the shape of a huge eagle, its red eyes glaring down at them in fury.

"We shall never escape!" cried Jeannie in despair.

But Mary remembered the words of her new friends, the tinker and the beggar. "A pure heart is never afraid," the tinker had said. "Gold and silver will save you from evil," the beggar had told her.

She took from her bag the gold needle that her mother had given her and turned fearlessly to face the eagle.

As he swooped close, his huge claws open to seize her, Mary thrust the gold needle deep into his heart. At that moment the eagle changed back into the wizard, and he fell, never to rise again.

His evil spell was broken. For a moment all was silent. Then one by one, birds began to sing on the hillside, and all the girls that the wizard had stolen came out of the castle, free to live their lives once more.

Mary and Jeannie went home to their parents, who were very happy to see their daughters safe and sound again.

Jeannie was still the most beautiful girl anywhere in the Border country—but never again did she go out to wash her face in the early morning dew!

Robin Hood

Robin Hood is one of the most popular of all English heroes, though no one is *quite* certain just when and where he lived. It is thought that he lived near Nottingham at the end of the twelfth century, one of the last Saxons still fighting the Normans who had conquered Britain in 1066. He robbed the rich to help the poor, and he was supposed to be the greatest archer of all time.

       *   *   *   *   *   *

As young Robin of Locksley walked through the forest on his way home, he could smell wood smoke. Not far away, something was on fire.

"It must be a big fire!" he thought. He climbed

a hill, and could see that the smoke came from the far side of the valley near his home.

Quickly he ran down the steep hill, then cut through the forest. He ran alongside the stream until he came to the lane, then, as he crossed the lane, he found Much the Miller's son sitting at the foot of the hedge.

"What's happening?" asked Robin, looking down at his friend. "I've been away for the last week, and it looks as though Locksley is on fire."

"The Normans are here," said Much. "Your rent was one day late, so they have taken your land, and they are burning down Locksley Hall."

Robin went white with rage as his friend spoke, and without further words they hurried on to Locksley Hall together. Watching from the edge of the forest, they saw that the whole house was on fire. Four of Robin's men were outside the stables, their hands tied behind them.

A tall Norman soldier walked over from the burning hall. He stopped in front of the four men— and drew his sword.

Silently Robin fitted an arrow to his bow and took aim. Before the Norman could strike, he was dead himself, an arrow through his heart.

Robin and Much ran across the grass, and quickly
cut the ropes which tied up the four men.

"Follow me," whispered Robin, and led the way
into the forest.

They stopped at last, a long way from the
burning hall.

"The Normans have taken my home, and I have
killed one of their men," said Robin. "From now
on, I'm an outlaw, with every Norman against me."

"We'll be outlaws with you," said Will Scarlet.
"We too have no homes any more; the Normans have
burnt them to the ground."

So that night, there was a new band of outlaws
in Sherwood Forest. They lit a fire to warm
themselves, and one by one they fell asleep.

Robin Hood and Little John

Deep in Sherwood Forest, Robin Hood and his band
of outlaws were safe. Almost every day, yet another
man would make his way through the forest and ask
to join them.

It was not an easy life, and many returned home
after a short time.

The outlaws lived in caves, or shelters made
from the branches of trees. Their only food was
what the forest could provide.

Each man spent part of every day in learning
to use the sword, longbow, and staff. They learned,
too, how to pass through the forest without being
seen or heard. Only the animals moved more
quietly.

One morning Robin set off through the trees.
It was his turn to bring back one of the king's
deer. He walked silently and warily, keeping watch
for the Normans.

Suddenly he heard the sound of twigs snapping
underfoot, a little distance away. Someone else
was walking through the forest, towards him.

Robin stood still for a moment, then he walked forward round the bushes to the edge of a wide stream.

On the other side stood a very tall man, who looked immensely strong. A bridge, made from the trunk of a tree, lay across the stream between the two men. Robin started to cross, and at the same instant, the tall man set foot on the bridge.

They stopped and looked at each other.

"Surely you saw I was already on the bridge before you started to cross!" said Robin.

"Go away, little man, or I will tip you into the stream," replied the stranger.

Neither would give way.

"If I had a staff in my hand like yours, I would soon teach you a lesson!" said Robin.

"Then get one from the forest, and I will show you how to fight!" replied the man.

Robin went back to the bank, and from a tree he cut a strong, straight staff. He trimmed off all the twigs and leaves, then went back to the bridge.

"*Now* let's see who is going to swim in the stream!" he shouted.

Backwards and forwards they fought, on the narrow, slippery bridge, with every step likely to land them in the stream.

The big man was surprised to find that Robin was every bit as strong as he was, and just as good with the staff.

At last Robin hit the stranger on the chest, drawing blood, but at that same moment the stranger's staff caught him on the side of the head. Robin was knocked into the water, and he disappeared from view.

"Where are you?" shouted the tall stranger.

"Here," replied Robin, pulling himself out on to the side of the stream.

The stranger came over and held out a long arm to help Robin up the steep bank.

"Thanks," said Robin, and they shook hands.
"Where are you going?" he asked.

"Nowhere. I'm running away because my master
treated me badly. He told his men to beat me, so
I ran away."

"What's your name?" asked Robin.

"John Little," replied the tall man—a strange
name for so large a man!

"It's nearly supper time," said Robin.
"Are you hungry?"

John Little nodded, and Robin blew three loud
notes on his hunting horn to summon the outlaws.
They soon arrived, and looked at Robin's wet clothes
in surprise.

"What happened to you?" asked Much the
Miller's son.

43

Robin told them about the fight on the bridge. Then he turned to John Little and said, "We are outlaws, living in Sherwood Forest—and you have no master. Will you join us, John Little?"

The big man smiled as he looked back at Robin. "Yes, I would like to," he said.

Robin clapped him on the shoulder. "Then you are now a member of our band. But we will have to change your name. From now on, you will be known as Little John."

The outlaws laughed and cheered, and that is how Little John came to join Robin Hood and his band of Merry Men.

Robin Hood and Friar Tuck

In the heart of Sherwood Forest, Robin Hood watched his men. At one end of the glade, six men were fighting with staffs, and other men were having an archery contest. With every day that passed, the outlaws grew more skilled.

Today a thin hazel stick had been stuck into the ground, and a bright yellow dandelion had been put on top of it.

As arrow after arrow landed beside the hazel stick, the men looked back at Robin.

"Come, show us how to shoot," called Will Scarlet.

Robin fitted an arrow to his bow and took aim. The arrow removed the dandelion flower from the stick.

"Let's see you do that again!" cried Little John.

Robin's second arrow split the hazel stick in two.

"I only know one other man who can shoot as well as that," said Little John, as the men cheered.

"Who?" asked Robin.

"Friar Tuck."

"A monk who can use a bow and arrow?" asked Robin, surprised. "I should like to meet him."

"He lives near the Abbey, a long way from here. He is a very strange monk—he was sent away from the Abbey because he threw the Abbot into the duck pond!" chuckled Little John. "I stayed with him for a while before I came here."

"He sounds like a fine man to have with us in the forest," said Robin. "I must go and find him."

The next day Robin set off for the Abbey, with some of his men. After travelling a long way, they came to the edge of the forest, and there Robin left his men and went on alone.

In a little while he saw the Abbey, and just beyond, by the river, a small hut built of logs. At the edge of the river, a fat monk was sitting.

Robin crept up silently, and put the tip of his dagger at the monk's throat.

"Good day to you, Friar!" he said. "I wish to cross the river without getting wet. You will carry me across on your fat back."

The monk nodded without a word, stepped into the water and bent over. Robin climbed on his back and was carried to the other side.

As he slid from the monk's back, Robin was suddenly flung over Friar Tuck's head. He landed on his back, and before he could move, the monk's knee was on his chest and his great hand had torn the dagger away from Robin Hood.

For a moment they looked at one another, then Friar Tuck said, "And now, my friend, *you* will carry *me*—back to the other side."

Holding Robin firmly by the throat, Friar Tuck climbed upon his back. Bowed down under the

fat friar's weight, Robin Hood staggered through
the water. He thought of dropping the monk into
the river, but the fat friar's hand on his throat made
him think again.

When they reached the other side, Friar Tuck
slid off his back, grinning.

This made the outlaw so angry that with a single
blow he knocked the fat monk into the water.

From Friar Tuck came an angry roar. He drew
his sword as he splashed out of the river.

They fought to and fro on the slippery grass, the
sound of their swords ringing through the forest.
On and on they fought, until Friar Tuck suddenly
shouted, "Soldiers! Stop!"

Quickly finding his bow, Robin Hood sent his
first arrow through the armour of a soldier. Two
more arrows stopped two more soldiers.

"We need help," said the fat friar. He placed
his fingers in his mouth, and gave a long shrill
whistle. From his log hut came a dozen dogs,
barking and snarling.

With the dogs biting and snapping at them,
and Friar Tuck and Robin Hood attacking them with
their swords, the soldiers fought as best they could
until their leader shouted, "Run for it! Run for

your lives!" He had seen Robin Hood's men coming from the forest.

As the soldiers ran away, Robin Hood and Friar Tuck stood and watched them.

"Well done, Robin Hood!" said Friar Tuck.

"You know who I am?" asked Robin, smiling.

"I knew who you were when you made me carry you across the river!"

They laughed and shook hands.

"Friar Tuck, I have heard of you, and you have heard of me and my men. Now tell me, will you join us in Sherwood Forest?" asked Robin Hood.

"Yes, I will come," said the fat monk. "I should like that."

And so Friar Tuck went to Sherwood Forest to join Robin Hood and his men.

The Crested Curassow

The West Indies is a name given to a group of
islands in the Caribbean Sea, which is between
North and South America on the Atlantic Ocean
side.

There are many different kinds of people living in
the West Indies, all with their own colourful
traditions. The following stories however are from a
time when only one kind of people lived there—the
Carib Indians, from which the Caribbean Sea gets
its name.

*   *   *   *   *   *

When the people known as Caribs first made their
home in the West Indies, the animals had no leader.
They lived in the forest at the foot of Mount
Roraima.

There was Mapuri the wild pig, the Parrot, the
Chattering Monkey, the tiny Powis bird, the giant
Sloth who hung upside down and moved very
slowly, the Toucan with his long curved beak, and
the Jaguar with long claws and eyes that burned
like yellow-green flames.

Because they had no leader, the animals argued and squabbled and quarrelled all the time. There was so much noise and confusion that eventually they all grew tired of it. Even the Chattering Monkey wished for silence.

Mapuri the pig called a meeting, and all the animals met to choose a leader who would stop them from quarrelling. They met in a clearing, and soon the noise grew and grew until at last the Wise Owl cried, "Who will it be?"

The Chattering Monkey stood up and offered to be leader.

"I know all the forest and where to find food and water. No other animal knows the forest as well as I do," he said.

But the other animals knew Monkey too well. He was full of mischief and quick to quarrel, so they would not have him as their leader.

Now Parrot, who had been watching from the branch of a nearby tree, flew down into the circle of animals and said that he would be their leader.

"You talk too much," said Wise Owl. "You will be for ever making long speeches, even when there is no one to hear you."

So Parrot was not chosen.

Animal after animal offered to be leader.

Mapuri the wild pig was too selfish and never thought of others.

The giant Sloth was too lazy and spent most of his time asleep, hanging from the branch of a tree.

No one, it seemed, was just right.

For two days the animals argued. One after another they offered to be leader, but each time all the others objected.

At last Wise Owl looked up and saw the small Powis bird quietly sitting on a branch, listening.

"May I suggest," said Wise Owl, "that we choose the Powis bird to be our leader?"

"Oh no! No!" cried the Powis bird. "I don't want to be leader. Indeed, my voice is too soft."

"Then we shall have to be quiet in order to listen to you," replied Owl. "For he that has a quiet tongue has a wise head."

"Yes," muttered the Sloth, "and if you haven't got too much of a voice, then you will not be able to talk too much."

"Correct," snapped Jaguar. "You won't chatter too much. You can be our leader."

So the animals agreed that the Powis bird should be their leader.

And every evening, from that time on, in the
quiet hour before dark, the animals came together
to tell one another the events of the day.

The Monkey chattered about the many things he
had seen from the tops of the trees, while the Ant
whispered about what he had seen close to the earth.

The strong and the weak, the large and the small,
sat together in friendship. If there was ever a quarrel
among them, the Powis bird heard both sides and
settled the matter.

The only one who was not happy was the Powis
bird. He did not feel impressive enough, especially
when there was an argument between two fierce
animals.

"I have nothing to show that I am your leader,"
he complained one day.

Wise Owl sat thoughtful for a moment, then he said,

"That's soon settled. We'll make you a fine crest."

In a moment all the birds and animals were busy making a crest for Powis. So beautiful was it when they had finished that it seemed full of bright jewels. It suited Powis perfectly, and looked as if it had always been there.

Now he looked like a king, his new crest was so fine.

"We will have to give you a new name to go with your new looks," cried the animals.

"No, no, no!" cried the Powis bird. "If I have a new name, how will my family know me?"

"That's not difficult," said Wise Owl. "We will give you a new name, but you can keep the old name too. We will call you Powis amongst ourselves but in the world of men you will be known as the Crested Curassow."

And all the animals shouted and cheered, and cried, "Long live Powis, the Crested Curassow!"

The Story of Kikushie

Jaguar was the biggest and fiercest of all the animals
who lived in the forest at the foot of Mount Roraima.

When he lost his temper and roared, the other
animals were afraid of him. He did not often go to
their evening meetings, and when he did, he took
little notice of their leader Powis, the Crested
Curassow.

After all, Jaguar had claws like shining steel, and
his roar echoed through the forest, and his body
was rippling muscle—and although Powis had a
beautiful crest, he was only thin, and covered with a
handful of feathers.

One night, when Jaguar did not bother to turn up
to their meeting, Mapuri the pig said,

"You know, Jaguar needs teaching a lesson!"

"And who's going to do that?" asked Monkey.
"Jaguar is strong and has sharp teeth!"

The next night Jaguar came to the meeting, but
he looked angry. His eyes flashed, and the flick of
his restless tail showed the tenseness of his body.
He had no wish to stay and listen to the tales of the
other animals. He had no wish to listen to idle
chatter. The forest called him. He snarled so fiercely

that the bright-eyed Parrot almost fell from his perch on a branch.

"I will stay here no longer," snarled Jaguar impatiently. "I need meat to eat."

The other animals shivered. What could they do? Jaguar was too strong for them to argue with.

Just then the animals saw Powis, the Crested Curassow, lift his head. His voice was quiet and his manner calm as he said,

"If the time of evening is the time when you like to kill, then go, but I pray that the fate which befell Kikushie may not overtake you."

The Jaguar was on the point of bounding away when he paused, and looked back. "Kikushie? Kikushie? Who was Kikushie?" he asked.

"Oh, surely you remember that? Kikushie was a relative of yours, many many years ago," replied Powis quietly.

"Yes," said Wise Owl. "I remember him. It was a pity . . ."

"What was a pity?" asked Jaguar.

"Poor Kikushie," muttered Powis, shaking his head.

"Kikushie? I don't remember any relative called Kikushie. What happened to him?" demanded Jaguar.

"Well, if you will sit quietly, I will tell you," said Powis. "I can't talk if you stand there flicking your tail about, looking angry."

With an impatient sigh, Jaguar sat.

"Of course," said the Crested Curassow, "the story that I am about to tell you was told to me many years ago by my grandfather, and *he* heard the story from *his* grandfather. So it is very old, but I can remember it clearly."

"Silly old fool, talking about grandfathers," muttered Jaguar beneath his breath.

Powis took no notice of Jaguar's bad manners, and began,

"Long, long ago, men and animals lived in peace, but they were afraid. Kikushie the Jaguar lived high on the side of a mountain, and every evening he would leave his cave and hunt for dogs and deer and wild pigs, and even the Caribs themselves. He would wait for the men who lived in the villages, and when darkness fell, he killed them.

"Kikushie's mate lived with him. One night he said to her, 'You go hunting tonight, I'm tired. I saw a Carib tie up a nice fat cow near his home in the village. That would make us a fine dinner!'

"So Kikushie's mate went off, but she did not come back. She was not such a good hunter as Kikushie, and the Caribs saw her and shot her.

"After this, Kikushie became fiercer than ever, for he guessed what had happened. Evening after evening, he raided the Carib villages, sometimes killing a man, and sometimes killing an animal.

"At last the Caribs called a council of war. 'This must stop!' they cried. 'It cannot go on. We are all in danger. We must make a plan.'

"So three hundred Carib warriors armed themselves with bows and poisoned arrows, and after dark on the night of a full moon, they surrounded the cave and waited.

"All was quiet, save for the sound of the wind in the treetops. When Kikushie left his cave and the scent of the Caribs reached him, he bared his teeth and snarled. He was terrifying, but the Caribs did not run away.

"The Carib chief shouted, 'Now!' and a cloud of arrows whistled through the air. Kikushie sank to the ground, dead. How the Caribs rejoiced! They were free from terror.

"To celebrate, they painted pictures on the wall of Kikushie's cave, and every Carib took a white stone and placed them in a row leading to Kikushie's grave."

The Crested Curassow stopped talking, then he slowly turned his head and spoke to Jaguar.

"To this day you will find that row of stones, and the paintings on the cave walls."

He paused, then said, "That's the end of my story. Well, off you go hunting, Jaguar."

"No," snarled Jaguar, but much less fiercely than usual. "I'll stay here."

And Powis the Crested Curassow smiled quietly to himself.

Mikel and his New Wife

Every country has its tales of smooth-talking strangers who take advantage of innocent country folk. This one, with its dry humour, comes from Austria.

⭐   ⭐   ⭐   ⭐   ⭐   ⭐

When Jan the farmer died, his gentle widow grieved for him for many months. Then after a year, she married Mikel, another farmer who owned land in the river valley.

She helped him on the farm, and each morning they would set out soon after daybreak to work in the fields. The work was never easy, and in the long hot summers it became really hard.

One day when the sun was high in the sky, Mikel said to his wife, "It's time to stop for a while. It's much too hot to go on working. I'll take the horse to the river for some water, and you rest in the shade."

He unhitched the horse and led it away down the field, and his wife made her way to some trees beside the road.

It was much cooler beneath the trees, and she heaved a sigh of relief as she sat down on a fallen log.

She had been working for many hours, and was very tired. For a moment or two, she closed her eyes and simply rested.

When she opened her eyes a few minutes later, she was surprised to see a stranger standing in front of her.

"Good morning," he said, smiling down at her.

"Good morning," she replied. "I didn't see you coming. Have you travelled far?"

"A long way. A *very* long way," he replied. "I've come from the other world."

"From the other world!" she said, astonished. "Well, fancy that! Have you met Jan, my first husband, there?"

"Oh yes," said the stranger. "He's a good friend of mine. He lives quite near to me, as a matter of fact."

"How wonderful!" said the woman, clasping her hands together. "Is he happy? Is Jan happy in heaven?"

The stranger hesitated for a moment, then he said, "Well, yes, I *think* he is happy."

"There's something wrong, I can tell," said the woman, looking up at him. "How can Jan be unhappy in heaven?"

"Well, it's like this," said the stranger. "He didn't take any money with him, and he's missing the little pleasures of life, like a cup of coffee from time to time, and tobacco for his pipe. I'm really sorry for him sometimes," said the man sadly, shaking his head.

"My poor Jan, with no tobacco! He always liked to smoke his pipe," said the woman. She took a handkerchief from her pocket to wipe away a tear as she spoke. "Poor Jan!"

For a moment she sat thinking about her first husband, feeling sad. Then she had an idea. "When will you see him again?" she asked.

"Soon. Very soon!" replied the stranger.

"Could you take him some money from me?" asked the woman.

"I'm always glad to help my friends," said the stranger. "I'll take it with pleasure."

"What a good man you are!" cried the woman, and without another word she went across to Mikel's coat, which was hanging from a branch of a nearby tree.

Reaching into the pocket, she brought out a purse full of gold. "Take this to Jan, please," she said, handing it to the man. He set off quickly along the road which led to the hills, and the woman watched him until he was out of sight. She went on sitting quietly on the log until her husband returned.

"Who were you talking to?" asked Mikel.

"A very kind and helpful young man," replied his wife.

"How did he help you?" asked her husband.

"He is a very special person," she said. "He has just come from the other world. And he said that he knew Jan, my first husband."

"In heaven!" exclaimed Mikel.

"In heaven," she replied quietly. "But he said that poor Jan is unhappy there."

"How can he possibly be unhappy in heaven?" asked her husband.

"He has no money, and he can't afford to buy the things he likes — a cup of coffee from time to time, and tobacco for his pipe."

Mikel was becoming suspicious. "And how was the young man so very helpful?" he asked.

"Well," said his wife, "I knew that you wouldn't want poor Jan to go without. I gave the stranger your purse, and he promised to give it to Jan as soon as he saw him."

Mikel could not believe his ears. "Oh, you did, did you?" he said grimly, growing red with anger. "And which way did this helpful young man go?"

"Towards the mountains," replied his wife, pointing.

Wasting no more breath, Mikel jumped on his horse and galloped along the road towards the mountains.

As soon as the stranger heard the sound of galloping hooves, he said to himself, "It must be that woman's husband!" He began to run as fast as he could along the road. When he came to a windmill, he ran inside.

Mikel was not far behind the stranger by this time, and he saw him run into the mill.

Inside the mill, the miller was filling sacks with freshly ground flour. He looked up as the stranger rushed in, shouting, "Run! Run for your life! The farmer's gone mad and he's going to kill you! Look!" The stranger pointed through the open doorway to where they could see the furious farmer galloping at top speed up the road. "You must escape!" he cried. "Give me your hat and take mine, then run for your life!"

The miller was frightened, and for a moment he could not think what to do. Then he exchanged hats with the stranger, climbed out of a window at the back of the mill, and ran off across the mountainside.

Quickly the stranger put on the miller's hat and threw some flour over himself. When Mikel rushed into the mill, the stranger was pretending to fill a sack.

"Where is he?" shouted Mikel.

"Who?" asked the stranger, looking surprised.

"The man in the red hat who came in here a minute ago!" thundered the farmer, now very angry indeed.

"Gone!" said the stranger, bending over the sack.

"Which way?" demanded Mikel.

The stranger walked over to the window and pointed to the figure of the miller, who was quite a long way away and still running.

"That's him! I recognise his red hat!" shouted Mikel. And muttering angrily, the farmer scrambled through the back window and rushed after the poor miller.

The stranger watched them both until they were out of sight, smiling a little to himself. Then he dusted the flour from his clothes, climbed on to the farmer's horse, and rode away.

Both the miller and the farmer were soon out of breath, for neither of them had run so hard since they were boys. Before long the miller could run no further, and he fell to the ground, puffing and panting.

"Now I've caught you!" shouted Mikel. "Where's my purse of gold?"

"What gold?" panted the miller.

"The gold you stole from my wife. The gold you promised to give to Jan, her dead husband."

"Gold for a dead husband?" exclaimed the miller. This man really is mad, he thought to himself.

The two men argued for a long time, but at last they both realised how they had been tricked.

Mikel rushed back to the mill, but the stranger and his horse were long gone.

Slowly the farmer walked back to where his wife was waiting for him in the fields.

"You've been a very long time!" she said. "And where is the horse?"

For a moment or two the farmer said nothing to his silly wife. Then taking a deep breath, he said, "I wanted to be as kind to Jan as you have been. I went after the stranger and I asked him to give my horse to Jan so that he will be able to ride about in heaven."

"You are such a kind man!" cried his wife, and she kissed him gently on the cheek.

The Princess Rind

The Norsemen, or Vikings as they are often called, came from the Scandinavian lands more than a thousand years ago. They were fighting sailors who explored far beyond the limits of the known world. Their stories are of great warrior heroes and beautiful princesses, and very human gods who lived in a far place called Asgard, ruled by Odin, the all wise, all seeing, father of the gods.

*   *   *   *   *   *

One day an old woman came to see Odin, king of the gods.

"Why have you come to see me?" asked Odin.

"I have come with news of the future," she replied.

Odin looked down at the old woman. Her face had many lines on it and her skin seemed as thin as paper, but her eyes shone brightly.

"What news have you, old woman, what news?" asked Odin.

"News of great sadness, and great happiness. And news of your son Vali."

"I have no son called Vali," said Odin.

"But you *will* have!" said the old woman. Then she sat by Odin and told him of many things that would happen in the future. She told him about times that would bring great happiness, and of times of great unhappiness.

She finished by saying, "And you are going to have a son called Vali, who will help you. His mother will be Rind, the princess who lives in the north."

As she spoke these words, the old woman disappeared, and Odin sat looking at the empty chair where she had been. Then he sat thinking about the old woman and what she had told him.

In time, many of the things that the old woman had told him began to come true, and Odin remembered the other things she had told him.

So after a while, he went down to earth to find the Princess Rind. As he rode through the mountains of the north, he heard many stories about her. It was said that she was very beautiful, but she would not marry anyone. She always said, "No."

"This one," she would say, "is too fat." Or, "That one is too thin." Other men were too poor, too ugly. No one, it seemed, was good enough to marry her.

Her father the king thought that she would never marry.

"I am getting old," he said. "If you do not marry and have a son, then who will be the next king?" But the princess took no notice.

One day, the king heard that a great army was marching against his kingdom.

"Who will save us, who will save us?" he cried. "I am too old to lead my army any more. And there is no one else in the land to take my place."

At that moment, Odin arrived. When he was told why the king was so worried, he said, "Let *me* lead your army. I will win the battle for you."

Although no one knew that he was the great god Odin, he was tall and strong, and he *looked* like a leader. He led the army into battle, and the king's enemies were defeated. They never came back again.

The king was so pleased that he said, "As a reward, you can have anything that I can give you."

"There is only one thing I would like," replied Odin, "I wish to marry your daughter."

"You can ask her," said the king. "But you are not young, and I fear that she may say no."

The king sent for the Princess Rind and said, "This fine knight who has saved our kingdom would

71

like to marry you, my daughter."

The princess looked at Odin and said, "No! He's far too old!" And she turned away and walked from the room without another word.

Odin was angry, and he went away. The old king was sad to see him go.

A few days later, Odin came again, but this time he looked like a young man.

"I am a goldsmith," he told the king. "I have come to make you beautiful jewellery."

The king was pleased to see the things which Odin made. For the beautiful Princess Rind, he made rings and necklaces and other fine jewellery, with pearls and precious stones.

"How can I pay you?" asked the king.

"I seek only one thing," replied Odin. "I wish to marry your daughter."

"You can ask her," said the old king, and he sent for his daughter.

But the princess did not want to marry the goldsmith.

"You are young and you are handsome," she said, "but you are not good enough. The man that I marry must be a rich and brave knight, as well as young and handsome." And without another word, she turned and left him.

Odin went away, more angry than before.

The king was very sad, for he was sure that the princess would never marry.

Soon Odin returned once more, and this time he looked like a young rich knight. When he asked the king if he could marry his daughter, the king was pleased. This time, he thought, she cannot say no, and he sent for her.

The Princess Rind looked Odin up and down. It almost seemed for a moment or two that this time she might say yes, but then she spoke.

"It is true that you are young and handsome. Your clothes and your armour show that you are rich, and you seem to be a brave knight, but I will not marry you. I am going to marry one of the gods." And with those words she turned away.

"Stop!" shouted Odin. "You have refused me too many times." He raised his hand and cast a spell, and the princess fell to the floor.

Then Odin disappeared.

The king was very upset. He thought that the princess was dying. After a while she woke up, but she could not talk. All day long she sat staring from her window, with not a word to anyone.

All the wise men and doctors who lived in the

land were called to the castle, but not one of them could help the princess.

"She has lost her mind," they said. "Only the gods can help her."

Many weeks passed, and the princess grew no better. Then Odin came to the king once again, disguised as an old woman.

"I can cure your daughter," he told the king.

"Old woman, if you can cure the princess, I will give you anything you want," replied the king.

The old woman opened her bag, and brought out herbs and sweet-smelling flowers. "Leave her with me. I must be alone with her or I cannot make her better," said Odin.

The king went away and left them together. Then Odin placed his hand on the head of the princess, and she was cured.

"Princess Rind," said Odin, "tell me about the man you wish to marry."

"Why should I tell *you*, old woman?" she replied.

"Because I can help you. You would not marry me when I led your father's army because I was too old," said Odin. "And you would not marry me when I was a young and handsome goldsmith, or when I was a rich brave knight."

The princess stared wonderingly at the old woman who stood before her.

"*Now* will you marry me?" asked Odin. And as he spoke, he took his own shape before her as Odin, the all-wise god of Asgard. "Will you be the wife of a god?"

The princess fell on her knees before him. "Yes, yes, yes!" she said.

She married Odin, and later, when their son Vali was born, her father the king was happy to know that there would be someone to follow him as king.

Thora's Dragon

Once upon a time, in the far north, there lived a
rich Viking chief called Herraud. He had a gentle,
beautiful daughter called Thora, whom he loved very
much. He could refuse her nothing, and when she
asked for a little house of her own, he had one built
for her, close to the family house.

He sent her a little gift each day—one day a
pretty shawl, another day a puppy, and another day
perhaps a bright ring for her finger—and each day
Thora looked forward to seeing what new gift her
father had thought of.

Then one day, when he was out hunting, chief
Herraud found a little green dragon. It was a pretty
thing, and he thought at once of his daughter. She
would love it!

Thora was very pleased with the little dragon.

She made a nest for it in a wooden box, and fed it with her own hands.

For a while the little green dragon slept in the wooden box, and seemed happy to be petted. But it grew quite quickly, and soon the wooden box was too small for it, so the dragon climbed out and lay beside the box.

Months passed, and it grew big enough to coil itself right round the box. Thora was happy to see her little dragon growing so quickly, and she loved to see its bright eyes watching.

Then the dragon grew even bigger, and lay round the walls of the room instead. Soon it was long enough to lie all round the room, its head touching its tail. When Herraud came to visit his daughter, he had to step over the dragon to get into the room.

"Isn't that dragon getting a bit *too* big?" he asked. "Do you really want to keep it?"

"Oh yes, father!" Thora answered. "No one else has a dragon like mine, and he's my pet!"

Herraud could never say no to his daughter, so he allowed her to keep it.

Then the dragon grew so big that the room was too small for it, and Thora found it one day lying outside the little house.

It went on growing and growing, and at last it could lie all around the little house, with its head touching its tail.

Now the dragon was so big and strong that no one could go into Thora's little house until the dragon would let them. And soon the matter grew even worse—the only man who was allowed to go through the door was the man who brought the dragon its meat.

People were so frightened of the dragon that they stopped going to see Herraud, and Herraud himself was wondering how he could free his beloved daughter.

As each day passed, the dragon grew and grew, and ate more and more meat.

At last chief Herraud said that whoever killed the dragon could marry his daughter, and he would give him land and great riches as well.

But even the bravest of the young men nearby were too frightened of the dragon to try their luck, and it went on growing steadily, eating more and more meat.

Then a young man called Ragnar, who lived on a distant island, heard about the dragon. He heard, too, of how gentle and beautiful Thora was, and he made up his mind to kill the dragon so that he could marry her.

He knew the dragon was very fierce, but he was a clever young man as well as very brave. He thought long and hard, then he made himself a very thick fur coat and trousers to match. He boiled the two garments in pitch, which was used to fill the seams in boats, and when he had finished, they were harder and thicker even than armour. His friends laughed at him when he put them on. They called him Ragnar Lodbrok, which meant Ragnar Hairy-breeches. He paid no attention to their laughter, for he knew just what he was doing.

Even as they laughed, he was examining the spear that he always used. He sharpened it, and half-pulled out the nail which held the head to the shaft.

His preparations made, Ragnar set sail to kill
Thora's dragon. He sailed for two days, then
anchored in a sheltered bay not far from Herraud's
house.

Early on the third day, before the sun rose, he
went to Herraud's house, wearing his thick hard
clothes and with his spear at the ready.

He could see the dragon's fiery breath in the dark,
and he moved so quickly and quietly that he had
struck his first blow before the dragon even knew he
was there. With his second blow he killed it, and

because he had half-pulled out the nail in the shaft, his spearhead came loose and stayed in the dragon's body.

As the dragon died, it roared and thrashed around in pain, so that Herraud and his men came running, but Ragnar had already gone.

Thora however had caught sight of him through her window, and had wondered who the brave young man was, for he was handsome, even though his clothes were so strange.

Her father was very glad the dragon was dead and his daughter was free. Thora told him she had seen the man who had killed it, but he was someone she had never seen before.

As he stood looking at the dead dragon, Herraud saw that the spearhead was still in the wound. He pulled it out, then called a council of all the men in the neighbourhood, to find out who had killed the great beast.

When they met together, Herraud told them that the dragon was now dead. The reward for the man who had killed it was Thora's hand in marriage, but he had not yet claimed her.

Then Herraud showed them the spearhead. "If any amongst you has a shaft to fit this spearhead, that

man has won my daughter," he said.

The men raised their spears—and every one was complete with a spearhead. Then Ragnar, who as a stranger had stood to one side, showed the shaft that he carried.

The spearhead fitted exactly, even to the hole where the nail had been.

Now Thora came forward, pleased to see the handsome hero who had won her hand, and Ragnar saw that she was indeed gentle and beautiful.

Then a great feast was held to celebrate the death of the dragon. Thora and Ragnar were married amidst much rejoicing, and lived happily ever after.

Prince Liam

Long, long ago, there was a king of Ireland who was
very greedy. He had many sons and daughters, and as
the time came for each one to get married, he tried to
find very rich husbands or wives for them. He
searched the length and breadth of Ireland, and each
of his children had to marry the person he chose, no
matter how ugly or bad-tempered they were. All his
children did as they were told, because they were
afraid of him. At last he had only one child left at
home—Prince Liam, the youngest—and he was *not*
afraid of his father!

When the king chose a very rich but very ugly old
woman as a wife for Prince Liam, he refused to
marry her. The king was very angry, for the ugly old
woman was one of the richest people in Ireland.

"Do as you are told!" he shouted. "Either you marry her, or you leave my palace for ever."

So that day, being a very stubborn young man, Prince Liam left home. He had no idea which way to go, but he set off westwards, and he walked until sunset. As dusk was falling, he saw a castle near the edge of a forest.

"I will call at the castle and see if they will let me stay the night," he thought to himself.

The castle was owned by a very rich man who was also sometimes lonely. He was delighted to see his young visitor.

"You are very welcome!" he said. "It is a long time since there were any young men in this house. Once I had seven sons, but they all disappeared when hunting in the forest. So now only my daughter and myself live here. Why don't you stay and work for me? You could help to look after my farm, and the workers."

"I will stay for at least a little while," promised the prince.

Next morning the rich man showed Prince Liam round his lands. He had a huge farm, with many fine meadows and woodland stretching as far as the eye could see.

When they were returning to the castle later in the day, the rich man said, "Tonight we shall have a feast. I want you to kill a really fat sheep—the fattest sheep you can find."

So saying, the rich man rode back to his castle, leaving the prince to search for the fattest sheep.

Soon after he had chosen the fattest sheep, he saw a tall beautiful woman walking towards him down the hill. By her side, on a chain, walked the largest dog Prince Liam had ever seen. It was a wolf hound. Liam felt that there was something strange about them as they walked towards him. "Can she be one of the fairy folk?" he wondered to himself. They seemed almost to float along, just above the ground.

When she reached him, the woman stopped. "Give me that fat sheep, and in return I will give you this wolf hound," she said.

"The sheep belongs to my master," replied the prince. "It isn't mine to give away."

"But your master will be very pleased with you," said the woman. "This dog is called Speed, and he can run faster than any other animal on earth."

So the prince gave her the sheep, and she went away, leaving the dog with him. Then Liam remembered that he had to find another sheep for the

feast, so he started to look for the second fattest sheep. No sooner had he found it than the woman appeared once more, again with a magnificent wolf hound on a chain.

She begged for the second fattest sheep in exchange for the dog, and again Prince Liam gave way. "This dog is called Strong," she said. "You will find him very useful. He can carry as much as anyone can put on his back." The prince bent down to pick up the dog's chain, and when he stood up again, the woman had gone.

By now it was beginning to get dark. He hunted once more for a fat sheep, but no sooner had he found one than the woman appeared once more. She had a third dog on a chain, which she handed to Prince Liam. "Take this dog," she cried, "and give me the sheep. This dog is the wisest dog in the whole world. He will be very useful to you."

She disappeared, and Prince Liam looked round at his three wolf hounds. He did not bother to look for any more fat sheep. Instead he took the dogs back to the castle, wondering what his new master was going to say. The rich man was not angry, however. He thought that the prince had made a fine bargain.

Prince Liam worked hard for his new master for some weeks. Then one day he said, "Tomorrow I should like to go hunting, with the three wolf hounds."

The rich man and his daughter were worried, for they knew it was dangerous. "Please don't go," begged the daughter. "Each of my seven brothers went hunting in the forest, and not one ever returned!"

Prince Liam however wanted to go hunting—and he was certainly a stubborn young man. Next morning early, he set off for the forest. Once there, he found the largest flock of birds he had ever seen, and he shot a great many, one after the other. His three dogs all helped him. Speed and Wisdom both brought the birds back to him as they fell to the ground, and Strong carried them all back to the castle. The rich

man was very pleased to see them all return safely
to the castle—especially with such a rich prize!

After that the young prince and the three dogs went
hunting in the forest many times. One day when they
were searching for birds, the dogs suddenly stood
still, raising their heads. Liam looked at them, and
stood still too. He listened hard, and in the distance
he could hear a crashing sound.

As the noise came closer, Liam saw it was a giant.
The giant saw Liam at the same moment, and he
raised his great cudgel to strike him down.

The three noble dogs sprang to Liam's defence,
and soon the giant lay helpless on the ground, the
dogs at his throat. "Help! Help! Help!" he bellowed.
"I will give you anything you want if you will save
me."

The dogs sank their teeth into him, and he bellowed even louder. "I will give you my castle and my lands. Help me, and everything I have will be yours."

Liam called the dogs to his side, and the giant slowly stood up.

"Now," said Prince Liam, "lead me to your castle —but do not try to escape or I will order my dogs to attack you again!"

The giant led them through the forest towards his castle, looking back fearfully from time to time at the huge dogs.

The castle was at the top of a hill—the most beautiful castle that Prince Liam had ever seen. Its walls were snow white marble, and the roof was made of gold. Inside, the walls were hung with rich tapestries and the ornaments were all of gold and silver. Wisdom padded in front of them through the castle, and Strong followed close behind, to see that the giant did not escape.

At last they came to a halt in front of a great iron door which was locked. Strong broke it open, and there before them they saw seven young men chained to the walls—the sons of the rich man!

As the door opened, the giant turned and ran. The

dogs chased him to the top of the castle, where he jumped over the wall to escape them. There he died.

The feast at the rich man's house that night was the happiest in the land. The rich man was pleased to see his sons once more. Prince Liam was pleased because the giant's castle now belonged to him. He asked the rich man's daughter to marry him, and she agreed.

When the wedding was over, Prince Liam returned to his castle with his bride and his three dogs. It was dusk as they came to the castle, and by the gate a tall beautiful woman was standing.

"I have come for the three wolf hounds," she said to Prince Liam. "I need them to help others as they have helped you."

Wisdom, Strong and Speed went off with her into the darkness, and they were never seen again.

Sova and the Devil

This is a folk tale from Yugoslavia.

★   ★   ★   ★   ★   ★

The moment the Devil caught sight of St Sova he
wanted to run away, for he always avoided priests if
he could. But this time, he could not. The path he
was walking down was very steep. To one side
was the steep face of the cliff, and on the other
there was a sheer drop into the valley below. There
was no escape for him. He would have to meet the
priest.

"God be with you!" said St Sova.

"I hope not!" replied the Devil in a surly voice,
trying to get past.

"Are you going far?" asked St Sova.

"That's my business," said the Devil crossly, as
the priest stood firmly in his way.

"Well, is there something you would like to do
that I can help with?" asked the priest. He was
so kind and good that he wanted to help everyone,
even the Devil.

The Devil sighed. He was not going to get past.
"I would like to grow vegetables," he said.

"Grow vegetables?" asked St Sova, astonished.

"Well, I would like to grow vegetables, but I can only do so if I have someone good to help me. Otherwise, anything I try to grow just shrivels up and dies."

"If that's what you want, then I will help you and together we shall grow vegetables," said St Sova, pleased that he could help.

"I don't like to work with priests," said the Devil, "but I know that you are honest, so we will share the work and share the crop," he said.

They talked together for some time, and at last they decided to grow onions. They bought the seed and planted it in a field which they rented from a farmer.

Soon the tiny onion shoots could be seen growing above the soil, and in a few weeks they had grown long and green.

"Now," said St Sova to the Devil, "this crop belongs to both of us. Half for you and half for me. Which half of the crop would you like?"

The Devil answered quickly, "I will have the part which is growing above the soil."

"All right," agreed the priest.

Soon afterwards the onions began to ripen, and the bright green leaves turned yellow and dried up. When the onions were ready there were only dead leaves above the ground. St Sova dug the onions out of the earth and took them home.

The Devil was not very happy, but it had been his own choice. He said to St Sova, "Let us try again."

"All right," said the saint. "What are we going to grow this time?"

"Cabbages," replied the Devil. "And this time you shall have the part which grows above the soil, and I shall have the part which grows underneath the soil." He really knew very little about vegetables.

"As you wish," said the priest.

So they sowed cabbages. Soon the big leaves

appeared. They were lovely to look at, and every day they grew bigger. The Devil was very pleased. The leaves were much bigger than the onion leaves had been.

"There is so much growing above the ground, just think how much there must be under the soil!" he said to himself.

In the autumn he watched St Sova cut off the cabbages, then with a crowd of people to help him, he went to the field to dig up the cabbage stalks. They all stopped to watch as he dug up the first stalk. Underneath there was only a dry root.

The Devil grew very angry because he was so disappointed. Then he went to look for St Sova.

"We will try again," said the Devil when he found the priest.

"Good," replied St Sova. "I do enjoy working with you. What shall we grow next year? Potatoes?"

"Yes, that's a good idea," said the Devil. "We will grow potatoes. Only next year I will have the part that grows above the soil, and you can have everything that grows underneath."

"I agree," said the saint.

So together the following spring, they planted potatoes. The weather was fine, and soon the green tops appeared and spread across the field.

"I have beaten the priest this time," the Devil said to himself.

But in the autumn the leaves turned yellow and died, and there was nothing left for him.

Then he watched St Sova dig up the potatoes which grew under the soil, and the Devil was so angry he could not speak for several days.

Then for the last time, he said to St Sova, "We must try again."

"I'm so glad. I do like working with you," said the priest.

"Half and half, as usual," said the Devil.

"Oh yes," agreed St Sova.

"This time I will have the half which grows underneath the ground, and you can have the part which grows above the ground."

"As you please," agreed the saint.

That year they grew wheat.

In time the wheat grew tall and straight. The ears of wheat formed at the tops of the stalks, and when it was ripe the priest cut it and took it home.

It was not long before the Devil saw that his share was going to be only the roots, and the short stubble that was left.

Then the Devil shouted with anger, and turned and stamped away. He never went near the priest again—and he gave up trying to grow vegetables!

Ananse and the Tiger

Stories about Ananse the Spider Man are told the world over, and translated into many languages. Most of the time Ananse is a man, but when he is in trouble, he can change into a spider. The stories came originally from Africa, where there are of course no tigers. In several parts of Africa, however, the leopard is known as a tiger—the Tiger of this story is really a leopard.

★   ★   ★   ★   ★   ★

Miss Melissa was a very pretty girl. As soon as Ananse saw her, he wanted to marry her. Then he found that Tiger wanted to marry her too.

Each day when Ananse went to call on her, wearing his best suit and carrying a bunch of flowers, Tiger was there as well. And Tiger was wearing *his* best suit and carrying a bunch of flowers!

They could never tell which of them Miss Melissa liked best. Some days it seemed that she smiled more sweetly at Ananse, and other days she seemed to like Tiger better.

Ananse began to think that Miss Melissa was going

to marry Tiger, and suddenly he had an idea. One day, when she was smiling at Tiger, Ananse whispered to her, "Why do you like my father's old riding horse so much?"

"Your father's old riding horse?" said Miss Melissa. "Don't be so silly. Tiger is not a horse. How could he possibly be your father's old riding horse?"

"When I was small, my father used to let me ride on him," said Ananse.

"I don't believe you!" said Miss Melissa, and turned away.

Later that day Tiger arrived, dressed in his best suit as usual, and carrying a bunch of flowers. Miss

Melissa smiled sweetly at him and asked, "Were you a riding horse many years ago? Did you belong to Ananse's father?"

"Of course I wasn't!" roared Tiger furiously. "Where did you get such a story?"

"Ananse told me," said Miss Melissa, "and he says it's true."

"I shall go and find him and bring him to you," growled Tiger. "And I shall teach him not to tell such a foolish story again." He rushed from the house in a great rage, roaring, "Ananse! Ananse! Where is Ananse?"

Ananse was quite a long way away, in his house, but he could hear the noise that Tiger was making. As Tiger drew closer and the roaring grew louder, Ananse locked the door and closed the windows. Then he hid in bed.

"Come out, Ananse! Come out!" roared Tiger, beating on the door. Then he kicked it until the hinges broke. He ran inside, and saw Ananse in bed.

"Get up!" roared Tiger. "Get up, and I will kill you!"

"I can't," moaned Ananse. "I can't walk. I'm so ill, I think I'm dying."

"All right," growled Tiger. "In that case I will

have to drag you to Miss Melissa's so that she will know what lies you have told." He pulled Ananse from the bed.

"Oh dear! Oh dear!" moaned Ananse as he lay on the floor. He groaned even more, then he rolled over on to his back. "I have pains in my legs, and my back aches. Tiger, I'm sure I am going to die. I have never been as ill as this before."

Tiger looked down at Ananse. It was true, he *did* look very ill. "If you are really dying, I must get you to Miss Melissa's as quickly as possible so that you can tell her the truth," he roared. He started to pull him across the floor towards the door.

Ananse cried pitifully, "Don't drag me any further!"

"Then start walking!" roared Tiger. "I'm going to make you tell Miss Melissa the truth. You are going to tell her that I am *not* your father's old riding horse."

"But I can't walk," sobbed Ananse. He rolled his eyes and trembled, like a man about to die.

"If you don't come, you will die anyway—because I shall kill you!" yelled Tiger furiously.

"All right, I *will* come—but you will have to carry me," moaned Ananse.

Tiger was becoming more and more angry. "Get on my back," he ordered. "I will carry you to Miss Melissa, and when you have told her the truth, I will kill you."

Ananse climbed on to Tiger's back—then he slid off the other side. "I can't stay on your back. It's too slippery," he cried. "If you put my blanket on your back, then I won't fall off."

"Oh, very well," grumbled Tiger. He went into the house once more, fetched the blanket, and spread it over his back. "Up you get!" he growled.

Ananse climbed on Tiger's back, and moaned and groaned as Tiger set off through the forest. Suddenly

he yelled, "I'm going to fall! I'm going to fall!"

"If you fall off, I will drag you!" Tiger roared
back.

"You will have to tie a piece of rope round your
neck so that I can hold on to it," said Ananse. Tiger
found a piece of rope, and he tied it round his neck.
Ananse held on to one end of it, and for a while he
said nothing as they went through the jungle. Then
he started to complain again. "Oh dear! Oh dear! Oh
dear!" he moaned.

"*Now* what's the matter?" shouted Tiger.

"Please, please, Tiger, do stop," pleaded Ananse. "The flies are terrible, they are making me feel worse than ever. Do let me get off and go home to die!"

"You are staying where you are," growled Tiger.

Ananse went on moaning, then he said, "Please, Tiger, at least get me a little stick so that I can brush them off with it."

From a nearby bush, Tiger broke off a small branch with some leaves on it, and gave it to Ananse, who stopped moaning at last.

Tiger hurried on through the jungle, and soon they were within sight of Miss Melissa's house. Tiger was pleased to see that she was sitting on the verandah with some of her friends. Now everyone could learn the truth at the same time.

Just at that moment, Ananse gave a shout, and beat Tiger with the stick. He pulled at the rope and shouted, "Gee up! Gee up!"

Tiger was so surprised that he ran very fast indeed, trying all the time to shake Ananse off his back.

From that day to this, poor Tiger has never been back to see Miss Melissa. Nor has Ananse—for ever since that time he has had to hide in the heart of the forest, so that Tiger cannot find him to take his revenge.

Androcles and the Lion

When the Roman Empire was at its greatest, about
two thousand years ago, the Romans ruled nearly
all the known world. They were magnificent soldiers,
and put courage above all else. Their legends belong
with the world's greatest stories.

$$\star \quad \star \quad \star \quad \star \quad \star \quad \star$$

Androcles the slave sat in his little hut, his back
bleeding from the beating his master had given him.
He had a cruel master. All day long Androcles had
to work in the hot sun, dragging blocks of stone from
the quarry. He had so little to eat that his bones
showed through his skin.

There was no hope for Androcles, for he had been a slave since he was a boy. He could only just remember being sold in the market, ten years before. That had been when he had seen his mother for the very last time, too. She had been bought by a rich man to be a nurse to his children.

Androcles tried the door of his hut, but as usual it was locked. When work ended at nightfall, he was always pushed into his hut with a bowl of food, and locked in until dawn.

The next day, and the next day, and every other day after that would be the same. And he could not run away—the punishment for a Roman slave who ran away from his master was death.

Some slaves had kind masters, but Androcles had not been lucky. Sometimes he hoped that his master would sell him.

He finished eating his bowl of food, then lay down on the pile of straw in the corner and went to sleep.

The next day his master was in an even worse temper than usual.

"Faster! Faster!" he shouted. "You are the laziest slave I've ever known." Then he beat Androcles again and again and again.

That night the slave sat and cried. There was no

hope for him. He would have to escape. He knew that if he was caught he would be put to death, but even that would be better than staying where he was.

His master opened the door and threw in his bowl of food. The bowl broke and the food fell on to the floor. Androcles did not move. He left the food where it was on the floor.

As he sat there, tears lying on his cheeks, he saw a thin beam of light shining into his tiny room. The door was open! His master had forgotten to lock it!

Softly Androcles went to the door and looked out. Inside the house, he could hear his master shouting at his wife. In the moonlight, Androcles could see across the courtyard to the gateway into the street.

Keeping to the shadows and treading quietly, he slipped around the courtyard until he reached the gateway. Then, without looking back, he left his cruel master.

There were few people in the streets. Once or twice he saw a soldier, and waited until the street was clear once more before creeping from the shadows again.

Soon he came to the city walls. The great wooden gates were shut, and he knew they would not be opened again until the morning.

He hid in an old building until daylight. Then, as a merchant went down the street to the city gates, he followed—looking like one of the merchant's slaves. No one noticed him leaving the city, and soon he was in the open countryside.

He had never seen the fields and woods before, and he loved the cool breeze upon his face.

He was enjoying himself so much that it was a few moments before he recognised the sound of horses' hooves behind him. Soldiers were looking for *him*! The runaway slave!

Quickly he ran behind some trees, and watched the soldiers ride past. Frightened in case they found him, he stayed there all day.

From then on, Androcles hid and slept in the day time, and at night he walked on and away from the city. For weeks he lived on berries and plants that he found in the countryside.

Early one morning, just as it was getting light, he found a cave. Just the place to sleep in until night came. Soon he fell asleep, safe in the cool dark.

When he awoke, his hand touched something soft and warm. He opened his eyes and there in front of him was a full grown lion, its yellow eyes watching him, unwinking.

For a long time he sat quite still, until all of a
sudden the lion whimpered. It held one paw in the
air as if it were hurt. Then it whimpered again—and
held out its paw towards Androcles!

Very very slowly Androcles took the lion's paw in
his hand, and looked. There was a great thorn stuck
in the middle of the paw. As carefully as he could,
Androcles took hold of the thorn and pulled it out.

The lion gave another whimper, then it began
licking the wound.

Androcles could not escape, for the lion lay right
across the cave, licking its paw. When it had finished,
the lion looked at Androcles with its yellow eyes, and
then it licked him with its rough hard tongue. For a
time Androcles was frightened, but soon he saw that
the lion was friendly.

From then on, Androcles and the lion stayed together. Every morning the lion went out hunting, and when it returned it always brought him a rabbit or other small animal for food.

Then one day the lion disappeared, and when Androcles went out to get food, he was caught by a party of Roman soldiers. This time there was to be no escape. He would not be sent back to his master— he would be put to death.

In those days, people loved to watch fights: but someone always had to die. The fights took place at the Arena, and great crowds went to watch. Sometimes runaway slaves had to fight each other, and sometimes they had to fight wild animals.

As Androcles was taken to the Arena, he could hear the roar of the crowds, cheering and shouting for blood. He grew more and more frightened as he waited for his turn to die—would he fight another slave, or would it be a wild animal? Then the door opened and a soldier pushed him out on to the floor of the Arena.

High above him the people watching grew quiet, wondering if he would put up a good fight, or if he would die easily. Then Androcles turned quickly to see an angry lion run from its cage. The lions were

kept hungry so that they were fierce.

Androcles backed away, and the lion followed him.
As it crouched for the death spring, its tail lashing,
Androcles closed his eyes. The crowds were silent,
waiting. This was what they were here for!

Then the lion padded over and licked Androcles,
and the Arena was so quiet that everyone could hear
the rasp of its rough tongue. Androcles gasped and
opened his eyes. When he saw his friend's yellow
eyes looking back at him, he threw his arms round the
lion's neck and hugged it.

The crowd looked on in wonder and astonishment
for a moment, then they began to cheer. Never before
had anything like that been seen in the Arena.

Such a wonderful thing had never even been heard
of before. Because it was such a strange and interesting
story, Androcles and the lion were freed, and they
lived together in friendship for many years afterwards.

Superman

Deep in the heart of Africa, there once lived a man who thought that he was the strongest man in the world.

And he *was* strong. When he went into the forest, he carried more wood than ten other men, and once when he found a dead tree, he carried it home on his head.

Each night when he got home, he would shout to his wife Shetu, "Come and see what your superman has brought you today!"

Shetu would smile gently and say, "You are certainly strong, but you are not superman."

This made her husband angry, and he would shout, "I *am* superman. Just show me a man who is stronger than I am!"

One day Shetu went to a nearby well for water. She had never gone to that well before, and she did not know it was a magic one. When she threw the bucket down into the well, she could not pull it up again, although she tugged and pulled for a long time.

At last she sat down on the ground beside the well and rested.

"It would take ten men to pull up that bucket!" she said to herself. Once again she tried to pull it up, but it was no use. She could not move it.

Sadly she began to walk home with her water jug empty, and just then another woman came by, a small boy on her back.

"Why are you going home with an empty water jug?" asked the woman.

"Because I cannot raise the bucket from the well," said Shetu. "It needs at least ten men to pull it up!"

The other woman said, "Come with me, and I will get water for you."

Then she took the small boy from her back and told him to pull up the bucket from the well. He took the rope in his hands—and up came the bucket, full of water.

The boy's mother filled all the water jars, and the two women set off home.

Just before they came to the village, the woman with the small boy turned to walk along a path on the left-hand side of the track leading to the village.

"Is your home along that path?" asked Shetu, surprised. "I did not know that it led to a village."

"Yes," replied the woman. "I live along here with my husband, Superman!"

When Shetu got home, she told her husband all that had happened at the well.

At first he did not believe her. Then when he saw that she was speaking the truth, he became angry.

"So there is another man who thinks he is Superman, is there? Well, just let me see him and I'll show him who is the *real* Superman!" he said.

"No, no, no," said his wife, frightened. "Keep away from him. He will kill you. His baby son is just as strong as you, so his father must be fifty times stronger."

Her husband took no notice. "Tomorrow you must take me to the path that leads to his house," he said.

So next morning Shetu took her water jar and led her husband to the well.

"First I must have some water," she said. There
at the well was the other woman, with her small boy
on her back.

"Give me that bucket," said her husband, and he
threw it down the well. When it hit the water he
said, "Now watch!" and pulled on the rope.

He pulled and pulled, but he could not raise the
bucket. The women watched as he grunted and
groaned, but nothing he could do would bring the
bucket up. He pulled so hard that he slipped. He
would have fallen into the well if the small boy had
not grabbed him and pulled him back.

The man sat on the ground in surprise. Then
he watched as the boy pulled up the bucket from the
bottom of the well, and the two women filled their jugs.

Shetu turned to her husband and said,

"*Now* do you believe me?"

"I still want to see this Superman!" shouted her husband.

So he followed the other woman back to her house. When they reached it at last, she said to him,

"My husband is out hunting in the forest. Hide in the corn bin, and then when he gets back you will be able to look at him. But don't let him see you, or he will eat you!"

"I'm not afraid," he replied, but he let her lead him to the corn bin, and he hid inside.

Towards evening the man in the corn bin felt the ground begin to shake, as Superman walked through the forest into the house. The man in the corn bin peeped out, and saw an enormous man, bigger than anyone he had ever seen.

"Wife, where is my dinner?" asked Superman, his voice booming like thunder. "Have you cooked that elephant I caught?"

The man in the corn bin could not believe his ears. It was all true. Here was a *real* Superman.

Shaking with fright, he sat waiting for the giant to finish eating the elephant his wife had cooked for him.

Just as he was finishing his meal, Superman began
to shout,

"Wife, wife, I can smell a man. Where is he? I
want to eat him."

"There is no man here," said his wife.

"I will find him!" said her husband. "I can smell
him plainly." And the house shook again as he
searched. Inside the corn bin, the man almost died
of fright.

At last Superman went outside to search in the
garden. When he had gone, the man climbed out of
the corn bin and began to run home.

He had not gone far before he heard a shout, "I
can smell a man!" and the ground began to shake as
Superman chased him.

The poor man ran faster and faster until he came to a field where some men were working.

"Why are you running so fast? Who is after you?" they asked.

"Superman is chasing me. Can you help me?" he asked.

"There are five of us here. Stay with us—we will stop him!" replied one of the men. But suddenly the ground began to shake as Superman came in sight. As soon as they saw him, the five workers went to hide, frightened.

So the man carried on running, with Superman behind him, until he came to ten men mending the road.

"Where are you going so fast?" they called in surprise. "Who is chasing you?"

"Someone called Superman is after me," he
replied.

"Then stay here; there are ten of us. We can stop
him," said the men.

The man stopped, but he knew what would
happen.

The ground began to shake as soon as Superman
came in sight. As soon as they saw him, the ten
road menders went to hide, frightened, and the man
began running again.

Now he was very tired, and he could not run much
further. Suddenly as he ran round a bend in the
path, he saw a giant sitting under a tree, eating
roasted elephant.

"Stop, little man," said the giant. "Why are you
running so fast?"

The man fell in a heap at the giant's feet. He could run no further.

"Someone called Superman is chasing me. Can you help me?" he panted.

"Of course I can," boomed the giant. "I am the Giant of the Forest, and I will help you."

Soon the ground began to shake, and Superman came in sight. The man jumped up and started running again.

"Come back," shouted the giant. "I will help you."

"He wants to eat me," the man called back.

"Come back and stand behind me," said the giant. "I will look after you."

So the man came back and stood behind the giant. In a minute Superman came rushing up and saw them.

"Give me that man," he shouted. "I want to eat him!"

"Try to get him then!" cried the giant, grinning.

So Superman leapt at the giant, and they began to fight. They were both so huge and strong that they were throwing each other to the ground, which shook as if there was an earthquake.

Then suddenly they leapt at each other at the

same time, and up they went into the sky, until they
disappeared from sight.

As soon as the man came to his senses, he ran
home and told his wife all that had happened.

Never again did he boast that he was Superman—
he had learnt his lesson!

As for the Giant of the Forest and the real
Superman, they are still fighting and wrestling high
above the clouds, and sometimes you can hear them.
People may tell you it is thunder, but you will know
that it is Superman and the Giant of the Forest,
because their fight is still going on.

The Sun Child

The Kingdom of Tonga, which is made up of a
number of islands, is in the South Pacific Ocean, and
is part of the Polynesian group. At one time Tonga
had a sacred king who had absolute power.

*   *   *   *   *   *

Long ago, when the world was young, a beautiful
girl lived on one of the islands of Tonga. She was
so beautiful and her father loved her so much that
he built a high fence round their home, to keep away
any young men who might want to marry her.

Thus, as she grew up, the only people she saw
were her mother and father, and her girl friends.
As the years passed by and she became a woman, she
did not even see her girl friends any longer, for
most of them were married and had children to look
after.

From far above the earth, the Sun God could see
the lonely girl, and he was sorry for her. Sometimes
he went to visit her at night, and he found out that
she was as clever as she was beautiful. The lovely girl
fell in love with the Sun God, and she married him,
although her father knew nothing of this.

A year later she had a baby son. Her father was very angry, but he could do nothing about it. The Sun God was one of the most powerful of the gods, and few people wished to arouse his wrath.

As the little boy grew up, the other children in the village began to tease him. "You have no father!" they shouted. So when the boy went home, he said to his mother, "The other children say I have no father. How can this be? Where is my father?"

His mother took him outside and pointed to the sun. "There is your father. He is the Sun God," she said.

After hearing that his father was the Sun God, her son would not play with the other children. "I am the son of the Sun God," he said, his head in the air. "I am too good to play with you."

Because he was so proud of being the Sun God's son, he grew up to be a very lonely young man. Then one day he told his mother, "I'm going to see my father."

Nothing his mother could say would stop him, and next day the young man set off.

For a whole day he walked towards the place where the sun rose. Then he came to the beach at the end of the island, and there he found a small boat. He dragged it down to the sea, and set off once more towards the rising sun.

He paddled all night beneath the stars. Then gradually the horizon became brighter until the edge of the sun appeared.

"Father!" shouted the young man.

The sun stopped. "Who called me? Who dares to call me father?" he asked.

"I'm your son!" shouted the young man. Then he told the Sun God about his mother, and about the island where he lived. "I want to stay with you," he finished.

"You cannot stay with me," said the sun. "Every day I must travel across the earth from east to west, or men will live in darkness."

"Will you cover the earth with clouds and stay with me for a while?" asked his son.

"Very well," replied the sun, and he covered the earth with clouds. "I will stay with you for a little while."

The Sun God and his son stayed together talking for a long time.

"I want to ride with you in the sky every day," said the young man.

"You cannot come with me," said the sun, "but if you stay here until it grows dark, my sister the moon will come. Tell her who you are, and she will offer you two gifts, one called Melia and one called Mona. She will tell you to choose one of them. You must ask her for the gift called Mona.

Don't forget—ask for the gift called Mona!" said the Sun God as he set off across the sky.

The young man lay down in his boat and went to sleep. When he woke up again it was dark, and the stars were shining.

He sat thinking. "It is clear my father does not want me," he said to himself. "But why does he want me to have the gift called Mona? Perhaps if I choose the other gift, I shall become like a god. Perhaps that's why he doesn't want me to choose the gift called Melia."

Slowly the sky grew lighter, and suddenly a shrill voice asked, "Who are you?" It was the moon.

"I am the son of the Sun God," replied the young man. "Have you got a present for me? My father said that you would give me a present."

"If your father said that, then I suppose I must," she replied. She held up two parcels. "This one is Mona, and this one is Melia," she said. "They look the same, but they are very different. One parcel has happiness in it."

"I want the parcel called Melia," said the young man. "Give it to me."

The moon did not want to give him the parcel called Melia. "Think before you choose!" she said.

"I know which your father wants you to have."

The young man became angry. "Give me what I want!" he shouted.

Sadly the moon handed him the parcel called Melia. "Are you quite sure that's what you want?" she asked.

"Yes!" he snapped rudely, and without even stopping to thank her for the gift, he paddled off in his boat.

When he was some distance from the moon, he unwrapped his gift. Inside there was only a shell, although it was different from any other shell he had ever seen. It was bright red.

"Why didn't my father want me to have this shell?" he wondered.

And as he wondered, he heard the sound of rushing water. He looked up and saw that small fish and big fish, whales and dolphins and even sharks were all coming towards him.

"Now I am truly a god," he shouted proudly.
"The creatures of the sea are all coming to me."

He stood up in his boat so that the fish could see
him and the red shell. They came up to the boat and
jumped high into the air, one after another, trying
to reach the shell. Many of them fell into the boat.

The splashing, wriggling fish filled the boat until
it sank, and with it went the proud young man,
still holding the gift he had chosen. He was never
seen again.

So he never knew that if only he had done as he
was told and chosen Mona, he would have become
a great chief and lived happily for the rest of a long
life.